Self-Suffic

A Guide to Growing Strawberries on the Smallholding

Two Classic Articles on the Planting and Cultivation of Strawberries

By

Various Authors

British Library Cataloguing-in-Publication Data
A catalogue record for this book is available from
the British Library

Fruit Growing

In botany, a fruit is a part of a flowering plant that derives from specific tissues of the flower, one or more ovaries, and in some cases accessory tissues. In common language use though, 'fruit' normally means the fleshy seed-associated structures of a plant that are sweet or sour, and edible in the raw state, such as apples, oranges, grapes, strawberries, bananas, and lemons. Many fruit bearing plants have grown alongside the movements of humans and animals in a symbiotic relationship, as a means for seed dispersal and nutrition respectively. In fact, humans and many animals have become dependent on fruits as a source of food. Fruits account for a substantial fraction of the world's agricultural output, and some (such as the apple and the pomegranate) have acquired extensive cultural and symbolic meanings. Today, most fruit is produced using traditional farming practices, in large orchards or plantations, utilising pesticides and often the employment of hundreds of workers. However, the yield of fruit from organic farming is growing – and, importantly, many individuals are starting to grow their own fruits and vegetables. This historic and incredibly important foodstuff is gradually making a come-back into the individual garden.

The scientific study and cultivation of fruits is called 'pomology', and this branch of methodology divides fruits into groups based on plant morphology and anatomy. Some of these useful subdivisions broadly incorporate 'Pome Fruits', including apples and pears, and 'Stone Fruits' so called because of their characteristic middle, including peaches, almonds, apricots, plums and cherries. Many hundreds of fruits, including fleshy fruits like apple, peach, pear, kiwifruit, watermelon and mango are commercially valuable as human food, eaten both fresh and as jams, marmalade and other preserves, as well as in other recipes. Because fruits have been such a major part of the human diet, different cultures have developed many varying uses for fruits, which often do not revolve around eating. Many dry fruits are used as decorations or in dried flower arrangements, such as lotus, wheat, annual honesty and milkweed, whilst ornamental trees and shrubs are often cultivated for their colourful fruits (including holly, pyracantha, viburnum, skimmia, beautyberry and cotoneaster).

These widespread uses, practical as well as edible, make fruits a perfect thing to grow at home; and dependent on location and climate – they can be very low-maintenance crops. One of the most common fruits found in the British countryside (and towns for that matter) is the blackberry bush, which thrives in most soils – apart from those which are poorly drained or mostly made of dry or sandy soil. Apple trees are, of course, are another classic and whilst they may take several years to grow into a well-established tree, they will grow nicely in most sunny and well composted areas. Growing one's own fresh, juicy tomatoes is one of the great pleasures of summer gardening, and even if the gardener doesn't have room for rows of plants, pots or hanging baskets are a fantastic solution. The types, methods and approaches to growing fruit are myriad, and far too numerous to be discussed in any detail here, but there are always easy ways to get started for the complete novice. We hope that the reader is inspired by this book on fruit and fruit growing – and is encouraged to start, or continue their own cultivations. Good Luck!

Contents

STRAWBERRIES.

Fragaria.

NO apology is necessary for introducing the consideration of Strawberry culture into a work primarily intended to discuss the profitable production of vegetables. True, the Strawberry is a fruit—one of the choicest and most popular we possess—but it is also an essential feature in most gardens, and fits in so admirably with the general crop rotation of market garden work, that its omission would be a serious mistake. In its season the Straw-berry is always in good demand, being a general favourite with both rich and poor, and although it is already produced in this country in enormous quantities, that fact need be no deterrent to laying down further plan-tations in suitable localities, providing its culture is entered upon with thorough-ness. At times and for short periods the markets are glutted with the fruit, but it

Royal Sovereign Strawberry.

is mostly of second and third rate quality, and even then the growers make its production pay very well, on the whole. There are never too many choice Strawberries offered for sale, the demand for them seeming insatiable. The grower who lays himself out to raise only the best fruit and to offer it for sale

1

in the pink of condition will find Strawberry culture to be one of the most profitable lines in his business; the more so if he extends his season by forwarding an early variety on the one hand and grows a breadth of a late variety on the other, and so evades the necessity of having to offer the whole of his crop for sale at the time of greatest general production.

Locality.—As indicated above, the locality of the plantation is a matter of the utmost importance—not necessarily in the production of the fruit, but in relation to its disposal. The Strawberry is a soft fruit and will not bear rough handling or close confinement in masses for more than a very short time. To be at its best it should be disposed of early in the same day it is gathered—almost before the morning dew has dried upon it, and whilst its bloom and brilliant colour are unimpaired. To secure this condition in perfection the fruit needs gathering soon after daybreak, packing immediately, and despatching by road to its destination, where it should arrive by 8 a.m. or soon after, without re-handling. If such an ideal situation is not possible, the next best is one in close proximity to a main line of railway, where there is a suitable service of through trains, preferably those with fruit vans attached. By this means the fruit can be put upon the market in good condition early in the same day it is gathered, with a minimum of re-handling and consequent damage from shaking and rough usage. In places where the railway service is direct but not convenient for delivery of the fruit early enough to be disposed of at that day's market, it may be made fairly satisfactory by gathering and packing the fruit when quite dry, before the evening dew begins to fall, and despatching it by a train which will ensure delivery of the packages soon after the opening of the market the following morning. The worst possible situation which can be selected for the culture is one remote from populous centres, from which there is no possibility of direct delivery by road, either to market or to shops, and where the only available outlet is by a branch line of railway. Under such circumstances the fruit, however carefully it may be packed, is frequently ruined by delays and rough handling; in the numerous changes of vehicles or trains to which it is subjected before it finally arrives at its destination, it gets so jolted and bruised that it is often partially reduced to a pulp, and if not also mouldy and altogether worthless (Strawberries under such conditions will go mouldy in less than twenty-four hours) the value of the consignment is so seriously reduced as to cause a considerable loss to the grower.

The Soil and its Preparation.—The best soil for Strawberries is one of a substantial nature—a deep heavy loam inclining to clay being generally the most esteemed, although it must not be overlooked that heavy crops of excellent quality are taken from plants growing on well-cultivated soil which is distinctly sandy or stoney. The fact is, that although the Strawberry will not thrive in a dry soil or climate, it will yield paying crops on any well-cultivated fertile soil which can be kept in a moist condition during the summer months—but, other things being equal, a heavy loam will give the best results, and should receive the preference for all but the earliest crops. The aspect of the land and composition of the soil have both great influence in determining the time of ripening. The chief points favouring earliness are—a soil of sandy composition with a porous subsoil, an aspect inclining slightly to the south or south-east, and plants of a proved early variety. Lateness is secured by planting on heavy cold soil, with a north or north-western exposure, and selecting a late variety. The grower should therefore make the best of his circumstances, planting the bulk of his crop to suit the formation of his land, whether early or late; if he has the choice of a variety of soils and situations he should make such selections and combinations as will suit his particular purpose, remembering that the more his season is extended in either direction, the more likely he will be to escape the losses occasioned by being obliged to sell on a glutted market.

Drainage should be attended to before a new plantation is made, and if not satisfactory it should be made so, for whilst the Strawberry thrives best in a moist soil, stagnant water is fatal to its well-being. The drainage being satisfactory, the next step is to work the ground thoroughly and deeply, incorporating well-rotted manure at the same time—it is of little use attempting to grow Strawberries for market in soil in a low condition of fertility. When the plants are to occupy the ground for several years, small areas should be bastard trenched and large areas subsoil ploughed, but when the plantation is only to be cropped for one or two seasons good ordinary cultivation will serve every purpose. Newly-broken pasture land is unsuitable; it should have been previously cultivated for at least one season, to reduce such pests as wire-worms, surface caterpillars, leather jackets and cockchafer grubs, which harbour in old grass fields, and also so that the soil, by the decay of the sod, may be brought into the compact condition in which the Strawberry thrives best.

For summer or autumn planting, the preparation of the soil should be completed as long as possible beforehand, so that it may become settled down before the plants are set out. For spring planting it is advisable, when possible, to ridge up the soil before winter, so that it may be made mellow and friable by the action of the weather.

Runners.—When the Strawberry plant begins to flower it puts forth long, slender, bare, cord-like branches, known as "runners." When these branches have attained a certain length their extremities become swollen and bear a cluster of leaves, and from the under surface roots are emitted. These roots enter the soil as soon as they come in contact with it, and thus the cluster begins a separate existence at a short distance from the parent plant. The runners do not end with the production

Strawberry Runner.

of one cluster of leaves, but each continues growing throughout the summer until four or five new plants have been formed in succession. If the runners are cut off the plant will produce fresh ones. All varieties are not equally prolific in the produc-tion of runners, some few being rather shy in this respect. In any batch of plants there are often a few " blind " ones— those which form neither flower nor fruit—and such are always fine looking plants with bold foliage, and are the most prolific in the production of early and vigorous runners; they should be searched for when the plants are blooming and destroyed, as plants propagated from them are likely to be barren also.

4

General Culture.—After a plantation is established, weeds should be kept down rigorously. Runners should be removed as fast as they appear, serious neglect in this particular being likely to ruin a plantation, and in any case when runners are allowed to grow they do so at the expense of the following season's crop. At all times during spring and summer, except when a mulch prevents, the surface soil should be kept in a loose condition by frequent stirring with hoe or cultivator; this will promote root action and ensure vigorous growth, the crop of the following season depending on the growth the plants have made in the previous year. After the fruit has been gathered and the runners removed, all the torn and withered old foliage should be carefully cut away, and with the litter and any other rubbish on the field, gathered together in heaps and burnt. In the autumn a mulch of rich compost or well decayed manure is given, and on large plantations a plough is then run between the rows, which puts the plants on ridges and keeps the roots well drained; in the spring a horse-hoe is used to level the ground again. Where horse labour is not used, *digging between the rows must not be permitted*, but in the winter a light forking over, about 3in. deep, will sweeten the soil and leave a friable surface to facilitate the work of hoeing. After the spring hoeing is done a mulch of long manure or clean straw is laid along the sides of the rows and between the plants to keep the soil from splashing on the fruit during heavy rains.

Strawberries do much better when grown by themselves, in an open situation away from bushes and trees, but sometimes they are grown between rows of young gooseberry and currant bushes, where they succeed fairly well for two or three years, until the bushes grow large and shade them; thus, they enable the grower to pay expenses until the bushes become remunerative. A plantation will usually bear well for three seasons, and it is even possible under good management to take fair crops from plants which have been established ten or twelve years. But it is very inadvisable to let them crop for more than three seasons, and many good growers turn the plants in directly they have borne two crops, and find this the most profitable method, the second crop usually being the heaviest the plants will bear.

When the production of extra fine fruit is the principal aim of the grower the plants should only be permitted to produce fruit once, digging them in immediately afterwards. The first crop, although not so abundant as the second, always yields the finest fruits, and annual plantations, as described later in the paragraph "Strawberries in Beds," will be found the best method to adopt in gardens where the soil is worked intensively, as not only are the individual fruits much finer, but from a given space the total crop is very much heavier than can be obtained by ordinary methods.

Few growers, especially those who produce the fruit on an extensive scale, realise the importance of irrigation when the fruit is swelling, particularly when the weather is dry; under such circumstances, when possible, copious supplies of water should be given, and will be found to greatly increase both the size of the fruit and the total weight of the crop. Where the plantation is inconveniently situated for giving water, a good mulch of long straw manure, along the sides, between, and partially over the plants, put on not later than the middle of March, will both feed the crop and keep the fruit clean. The foliage grows through fresh and strong, and by the time the fruit appears the straw is washed clean by the rains.

Plants.—The success of the plantation, both immediately and permanently, depends upon the quality of the plants used, and the importance of this fact cannot be too strongly impressed upon the inexperienced beginner in Strawberry culture. Where a plantation is being formed for the first time, the plants should be obtained from a firm of good standing and repute, who make the propagation of Strawberry plants a leading line in their business. The first cost of the plants will probably be a little more than would be the case if they were ordered haphazard from advertisers who offer them very cheaply, but it will be money well spent, and really far cheaper in the end, to make a start with good plants instead of with miserable, stunted specimens, gathered anyhow from fields which have been allowed to run wild; the misguided and unfortunate purchaser of such plants often receives them in the form of bags of sweating rubbish not worth the cost of railway carriage. The only plants fit for the intended purpose are those showing good growth, with plenty of leaves, and strong, abundant light-coloured roots; small stunted plants, small of leaf and sparse of root, or old plants with dark-coloured, withered roots, should always be rejected—they rarely become profitable.

The first runners from a plant are always the strongest as well as the earliest. Those from vigorous young virgin plants that have never been weakened by fruiting are still earlier and stronger than the best from the fruiting stock, and it is more than probable that if propagation from virgin plants was continued for some years a strain of any variety would be built up which would far exceed in vigour, healthfulness, and cropping powers that which had been propagated from plants debilitated by years of fruit production. That being so, and an annual supply of such runners being quite easy to obtain, it is strongly recommended that at least on those limited areas where the quality of the fruit is the principal aim, the following method be adopted: During the winter prepare a bed or beds, 5ft. wide and as long as necessary, by thoroughly digging and incorporating at the same time a generous dressing of well-decayed manure. Towards the end of March, when the weather has been fine for a few days, stir the surface of these beds, and put on a 2in. covering of rich compost or sifted old hot-bed manure, supplemented with a light sprinkling of sulphate of potash and superphosphates. Then carefully plant strong lifted runners or, preferably, plants from pots, in two rows 2ft. apart, and 18in. from plant to plant, closing the soil well around the crowns and making it very firm about the roots. Remove all blossom as soon as it appears. As runners are put out peg down the earliest ones from each plant until the whole of the space is covered with young plants at about 6in. apart, after which all others must be rigorously removed. If the weather is dry an occasional soaking with water will assist rooting very materially. As soon as the runners are rooted strongly separate them from the old plants. By the middle of July the young plants will be growing vigorously, and if transplanted to their fruiting quarters before the end of August—but the sooner the better—they will yield a good crop of large choice fruit the following season. At the same time sufficient runners should be planted 6in. apart each way in a nursery bed to make up fresh beds in the following spring for a further supply of plants, or they may be left where they are standing through the winter. The old plants, not yet having fruited, will yield a great crop the following season.

Summer Planting.—All things considered, the best time to make a new Strawberry plantation is early in August. This entails more labour than when the plantation is made either in autumn or spring, but if August planting is well done and the plants properly cared for afterwards, a good crop of fruit can be gathered from them the following season, whereas when planting is done on either of the other dates none can be had until the second season; therefore the additional labour receives an abundant recompense. One of the best crops to precede summer-planted Strawberries is early potatoes; the tillage and manuring which potatoes require cleans, aerates, and enriches the soil, and if it is harrowed and rolled after the crop is lifted it is in prime condition for receiving the plants. Some difference of opinion exists as to the best distance apart to set them, but much depends upon the vigour of the variety and the nature of the soil. A safe rule on the average is to set the rows 2ft. apart, and the plants 18in. apart in the rows, but some varieties are all the better for 6in. more space each way, whilst others need not be more than 1ft. apart in the row. It is a good plan to omit every third row for convenience of gathering and cultivation, as then there will be no need to trample amongst the plants, for although the Strawberry thrives best in firm soil this does not mean a bed almost as hard as concrete, which is the condition most heavy soils would be in when dry, if trampled on when wet. This space can be filled with lettuce or some similar crop which is cleared before gathering begins, and there is thus little or no loss. Dull cloudy weather, when the soil is moist, should be chosen for the work when possible, but do not plant when the soil is wet and pasty, or the roots will not run freely. Do not plant with a dibber, but use a garden trowel, and see that the roots are spread out evenly, then fill in with fine friable soil, which should be pressed quite firmly round the roots, further consolidating the earth by treading in afterwards. The collar of the plant when all is finished should be just level with the surface—not in a hollow or it will hold moisture and induce decay, and not raised above the surface, because the tendency of the plant is to rise out of the ground and this must be counteracted as much as possible. If the weather is dry, every

RIGHT AND WRONG WAYS TO PLANT STRAWBERRIES.

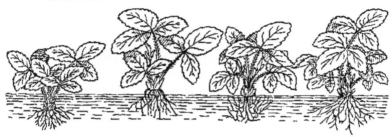

| Buried too deeply. | Not planted deep enough. | The proper depth but badly planted; roots turned up. | Well planted, at proper depth. |

precaution must be taken to keep the roots of the plants moist. A box is better than a basket to carry the plants in, because the wind cannot blow through the sides, and it should be kept covered with a wet sack. When the plants have been obtained from a distance it is always best, before planting in dry weather, to dip the roots in a " puddle " (a mixture of soil or clay and water, of the consistency of cream). On light soils, as soon as planting is finished, it is a good plan to run a light roller over the whole area—plants as well, it will not hurt them. In dry weather water should be given unsparingly until the plants are established. Weeds must not be permitted at any time, and the surface soil should be kept constantly stirred during the growing season with hoe or cultivator; this, as has been frequently mentioned, not only keeps the weeds down, but helps to retain moisture in the soil and keeps it friable and aerated, with the result that the plants grow more vigorously, and so make stronger crowns.

Autumn Planting.—When planting cannot be conveniently done in the summer, autumn is the next best time, providing the operation can be completed by the end of October; Strawberries may be planted up to the end of December in open weather, but it is very inadvisable to do the work so late, as the roots remain inactive in the cold wet ground, and it is almost certain that many of the plants will die and need replacing; therefore, if planting cannot be finished at latest by the end of October it is best to leave it until spring. Peas are one of the best crops autumn-planted Strawberries can follow; the ground should be broken up as soon as the haulms are carted away and the interval before planting allows ample time to get the soil into capital condition for the work. If the runners have been grown at home no more should be lifted than can be planted the same day, so that the roots will not get dried by wind. If they have come from a distance unpack immediately on arrival, spread out thinly in a shady place, and sprinkle lightly with water; if they cannot all be planted at once open a shallow trench on the north side of a wall or hedge and stand them thickly in this, covering the roots with moist soil. When planting time arrives trim off about one third of the roots with a sharp knife and remove all decayed leaves, then mark out the rows and plant as directed on pages 323-4.

Spring Planting has many good points which commend it to the favour of the busy grower, and there is not the least doubt that it is far better to plant in spring than late in the autumn. In spring the soil is cool and moist, the roots begin to work at once and the plants grow strongly from the start, so that there are very few losses. When this course is to be followed the runners should have been cleared from the fruiting plantations in autumn and heeled in on a bed of well-drained soil. Open a shallow trench wide and deep enough to take in the roots of the runners and so that the crown is just above ground level; stand them close together in a single row along one side, then open another trench, parallel with the first and about 6in. away from it, using the soil to cover the roots of the plants in the first trench. Cover the roots well and tread in the soil firmly so that every plant is bedded in tightly. Trenches may be repeated in this way until all the runners are disposed of, and they will then be found in first-rate condition for planting in the spring. The ground should have been well manured and ridged up in the preceding autumn, so as to get the full benefit of frosts in pulverising the clods and making the whole mellow and friable. After a few days of fine weather about the beginning of March, when the soil works well and is not wet or sticky, it should be harrowed down and levelled. Before planting remove any withered or dead leaves there may be on the runners and shorten the longest of the roots. The distance apart of the rows will depend upon the variety planted and the nature of the soil, but where horse-hoeing is intended it should not be less than 2ft. 6in. During the first season another crop may be grown between the rows, onions being a favourite one for this purpose. When this is the case two rows of onions, 9in. apart, are drilled in the spaces as soon as the Strawberries are planted. During the first season any blooms which show must be picked off as soon as seen and no runners should be allowed to form.

Strawberries in Beds.—Planting in single rows, as already described, is the customary method approved and carried out by the vast majority of growers; there is, however, a method of growing in beds, described below, which is worthy of serious attention from all who aim not only at the production of choice fruit but who also strive to "forward" a portion of their crop so as to have ripe fruit ready a week or ten days earlier than it would ripen naturally in the open. The method is simple and profitable, and if carried out thoroughly will ensure a heavy crop of fine fruit being taken off a comparatively small space.

The requisite number of good strong runners from maiden plants should be set out 6in. apart on a nursery bed, not later than September—the earlier the better. Here they remain until planted out permanently in the following spring. During the winter the land intended for the plantation should be bastard trenched—a good dressing of well-decayed farmyard manure being incorporated with the top spit at the same time—and thrown up into beds 5ft. wide, with furrows or pathways, 12in. wide and 6in. deep, dividing the beds. The surface of the soil should be left rough for the weather to act upon. About the end of March, when the weather is fine and the soil is in nice working condition, prepare the beds and set two rows of plants on each, as described for the propagation of runners on pages 322 and 323. Lift the plants from the nursery beds with a garden trowel, each with a good ball of earth. Keep the surface of the soil stirred by frequent hoeing, but do not cut in more than 1in. deep. Remove all blossoms as soon as they show, as the plants *must not be allowed to fruit.* When runners appear peg down the earliest until the whole surface, except a 9in. margin along each edge, is covered with plants 9in. apart. They must not be closer than this or the plants will be overcrowded and the size of the fruit will suffer in consequence. The beds should be kept moist by frequent watering until the runners are rooted. As soon as this has taken place *cut the old plants out.* Each bed is now covered with young, vigorous, early-rooted plants, which by suffering no check from transplanting make extra fine crowns by the autumn. No further runners must be allowed to form, weeds must be kept down, the surface soil stirred, and if the summer should prove very dry the beds should occasionally be watered copiously—preferably in the evening—so as to help the plants to make all the growth possible, the crop of fruit depending largely upon the growth of the preceding season. The furrows between the beds will remove all surplus water in the winter and in conjunction with the deep cultivation will keep the plants free from stagnant moisture and ensure healthy root action. When growth begins in the spring apply the fertilizers mentioned later. When the plants are in bloom dress the bed with good equalized guano, and *water copiously* until the fruit begins to show colour. The result will be a very heavy crop of extra fine fruit which will surprise the grower who has adopted this method for the first time and will repay him abundantly for all the trouble he has taken.

To perfect this system, a portion of the plantation should be brought to the fruiting stage earlier than it would otherwise be under normal conditions; this procedure is known as "forwarding," and is accomplished by covering the plants, as soon as growth begins in March, with movable box frames. The most convenient size of frame for this purpose is that described on pages 69-71, which will fit comfortably on the 5ft. bed with a margin of a few inches of earth on each side to give it a firm foundation. If the plants were kept 9in. from the the edges of the bed, as directed, the nearest will be a few inches from the side-boards of the frame. After the lights are put on ventilate freely, never closing them entirely except in rough or frosty weather. On no account let the plants suffer from want of water, but on the other hand do not over-water—the soil should be maintained in a nice moist condition suitable to free and uninterrupted growth. On the occasion of a warm gentle rain the lights may be removed altogether so that the plants may receive the full benefit of it. As the weather gets warmer raise the lights more and give a light watering over the leaves through a fine rose morning and evening. When the blooms begin to open this dewing over should cease unless the weather is exceptionally hot and dry. Fertilization of the flowers should take place daily, by brushing them lightly over with a rabbit's tail or bunch of feathers tied to the end of a stick; this scatters the pollen.

The plants on these beds, whether forwarded or fruited in the open, should only be allowed to bear one crop, and as soon as that is gathered the plants should be chopped out or dug in and the ground prepared for some other crop. A fresh plantation should be made each spring, and then each season there will be one in bearing.

The Forcing of Strawberries.—The preparation of the soil for forcing is a matter of importance and has a great influence upon the ultimate result. The principal ingredient should be good turfy loam, cut from meadow land if possible. This should be cut and stacked, grass side downwards, in the previous autumn, adding at the same time alternate layers of well-decayed manure—about one-fourth manure to three-fourths loam—and a sprinkling of powdered lime, bone meal, and kainit between each layer; if there are wireworms in the sod, one of the advertised wireworm destroyers should also be added to each layer. Make the heap fully large enough for the intended work, as any surplus will be found useful for many other purposes. Early in the spring cut the heap down, thoroughly mixing it and chopping up the turf with a sharp spade in the process. Stack it again and repeat the turning and chopping twice more at intervals of five or six weeks; the largest of the pieces then should not exceed the size of a walnut. The soil should be nicely moist and if not in this condition it must be watered well at each turning; liquid manure used for one watering will still further improve the soil. At the second turning sufficient should be passed through a screen to fill the pots for layering, the lumps being thrown back on the heap. For this purpose the soil needs to be in smaller particles than for potting at a later stage, so that the delicate rootlets may enter it easily. When there is an opportunity for doing so it is a good plan to fill the pots a few days before they are needed and then there need be no undue delay in getting them into position at the proper time. Before filling them soak the pots in water and see that the soil is moist; also be sure to provide sufficient crocks or other drainage material. When filled, stack them in a cool shady place, where they will be safe from the direct rays of the sun and also from rain; a few wet sacks thrown over them will help to keep the moisture in the soil.

Strong well-rooted runners of a good forcing variety should be lifted at the end of July and potted in 32's, either one or two to a pot; or they may be layered in small 60's, and after becoming well rooted, potted singly in 32's. When the runners are to be rooted directly into the small pots these should be sunk in the ground up to the rim, and so disposed as to leave a

Two Methods of Layering
Strawberry Runners.

Runner Layered into
a 60's Pot.

Runner Layered into
the Ground.

clear path between every two rows for convenience in giving water, which matter which must on no account be neglected. Do not take more runners from one plant than is absolutely necessary, and when possible confine these to one on a stalk, that nearest the parent plant being usually the best. Examine each runner before layering it to see that it contains a centre of embryo leaves; those without this centre are almost sure to be blind and should be discarded. Always layer enough plants in excess of the actual requirements to allow for losses and for rejecting poor plants. Having plunged the pot and selected the runner cut off the continuation of the stalk or "string" about half an inch beyond the tiny plant, then fix this on the soil in the middle of the pot. The fixing may be done in a variety of ways; in many places a lump of earth or a small stone placed on the string is considered sufficient, whilst in others forked twigs or bits of bent wire are employed; common hairpins are as cheap and convenient for the purpose as anything that can be used. Be sure that the soil is fairly firm in the pot and the runner pressed down upon it and fastened securely. The soil in the pots must be kept moist by watering daily, and as the plants grow and the pots fill with roots this attention will be required twice daily, especially if the weather is very hot, as it usually is in July and August.

When the runners are allowed to root in the ground the surface should first be well hoed and then covered with 1in. of old hot-bed manure, finely sifted, and the whole thoroughly watered. The same care and attention in selecting, pegging down, and watering will be required in this case as when pots are used, but watering will not need doing so frequently.

Early in August the runners should be ready for placing in the fruiting pots (32's), whether layered in small pots or rooted in the ground. In the latter case the plants must first be well watered and then lifted with a good ball of earth to each, only lifting so many at a time as can be potted immediately. Each pot must be provided with plenty of drainage material, carefully arranged so that water can pass away freely, as nothing is more harmful to the plants or more likely to cause the whole operation to be more or less of a failure than the presence of stagnant water, which causes the soil to become soddened and sour. A layer of the roughest pieces of soil should be put over the crocks, and then the pot should be partially filled, leaving enough space so that when the plant from the 60's pot or that with a ball of earth is placed inside, the collar of the plant will be about 1in. below the rim of the large pot, the crocks in the small pot having been first removed. Fill round gradually with soil, making it quite firm with a wooden rammer as the pot is filled, bringing the new soil about half an inch deep

over the previous surface, so that the crown of the plant just stands above it. Firm potting is essential to success; satisfactory crops of Strawberries can never be obtained, either from plants in pots or from those in the open ground, when the soil about the roots is in a loose condition.

After potting, set the plants on a bed of ashes, 2in. deep; this will prevent the entrance of worms into the pots and keep the drainage holes from being blocked by earth. Where sufficient box frames are available it is a good plan to stand the pots inside these, without lights; they can then be very easily protected

Section showing Proper Method of Potting Plant from Small Pot in a Large one.

through the winter. In any case the pots must be so arranged that pathways are left between them at intervals for convenience of watering. Shade from the sun should be provided for a few days to enable the roots to quickly begin working in the new soil. Dew the leaves of the plants over daily but give no other water until the shade is removed. They must then be exposed to the full sunshine and will need a good watering. They must now be attended to with great care; only moderate quantities of water will be necessary at first, but as the pots get filled with roots copious supplies must be given to keep them growing freely—sometimes twice a day when the weather is very hot—and a syringing every afternoon will be beneficial and keep them free of insect pests. Runners must be cut off as soon as they show and the soil kept free from weeds.

When the weather becomes cool and wet in the autumn watering must cease, and it will be necessary to provide some protection for the pots, or many will get broken by the frost. If the pots were stood inside box frames, as suggested, the lights can be put on and no further protection will be required

unless the weather gets very severe, when they may have an
additional covering of mats. In this case the lights should
never be closed down entirely except in hard frost. Where
no frames are available it is a good plan to stand the pots close
together, plunged up to the rim in ashes, the ashes being kept
in place by boards on edge round the outer margin of the mass.
In many places the pots are simply laid on their sides and
stacked on the top of each other, with a covering of straw over
the top layer; they do very well in this way except that the
soil is apt to become too dry and each pot needs soaking in
water before being taken in for forcing.

The first hot-beds for forcing are made, 2ft. thick, at the end
of January, according to the directions given on pages 128-130.
When the heat has fallen to 50 degrees put on the frames, put
fine soil inside, 2in. deep, and stand the pots on this, close
together, packing soil round them until they are all immersed
in it up to the rims. Give no water until growth begins, and
then very moderately, increasing gradually as growth becomes
stronger. Plenty of air should be given whenever the weather
will permit. Dew over the plants with water through a fine
rose every bright day until the bloom begins to open, when it
must stop for a time until the fruit is " set." In order that the
pollen of the flowers may be readily scattered, and so ensure
proper fertilization, the atmosphere inside the frame must be
kept as dry as possible during the blooming period, dampness
in the atmosphere being very detrimental to a good " set " of
fruit. During the same period, whilst avoiding cold draughts,
as much air must be given as the state of the weather will
permit, and the flowers must be lightly brushed over daily,
about mid-day, with a rabbit's tail.

During this time watering at the roots must not be neglected,
but it must be done carefully, avoiding wetting the foliage.
As soon as a sufficient number of fruits are seen to be set,
which will be in ten or twelve days after the first flowers open,
dewing over daily must be resumed, the atmosphere of the
frame now requiring to be kept moist to assist the swelling of
the fruit. The soil must never be allowed to become dry at
this period, and liquid manure should now be used alternately
with clear water. Give a little air during the day but close

down early in the afternoon. When the fruits are about half coloured stop dewing, give more air, and leave the lights slightly raised at nights if the weather is mild; a free circulation of air whilst the fruits are ripening will improve their flavour. The fruit should be propped up with forked twigs, to keep it from touching the soil. Mats must be used to cover the lights every night whilst there is any danger of frost. A fair amount of warmth must be kept in the bed, and to this end the sides and ends of the bed should be pulled down occasionally and the cold manure replaced with some that is fresh and hot, banking it up to the top of the frameboard.

About the third week in February another hot-bed, 18in. thick, should be made for a second batch of plants, and a third, 1ft. thick, early in March. These will carry on the supply until those being "forwarded" are ready. The last lot do better if turned out of the pots and planted directly in the soil, otherwise the treatment is the same in each case.

Varieties :—The following is a selection of a few varieties, all good and worthy of the market growers' attention, although the list is by no means exhaustive of the best. At the same time it must be remembered that some Strawberries succeed remarkably well in one situation and are very unsatisfactory in another; therefore any variety which has not been proved to succeed in a district should not be planted largely until it has first been tested on a small scale.

Early :—

ROYAL SOVEREIGN.—Fruit very large and firm, with a pleasant flavour; heavy cropper; vigorous grower, succeeding almost anywhere; *one of the best for forcing;* in great favour with growers for market; where only one variety is grown this should be chosen.

THE LAXTON.—This variety has all the good points of Royal Sovereign except that it does not force well.

NOBLE.—Fruit very large and handsome but of rather poor flavour; very prolific; vigorous grower, succeeding in most places.

VISCOUNTESS HERICART DE THURY (Garibaldi).—Fruit medium size, firm, and of excellent flavour; enormous cropper; robust grower; *forces well;* one of the best in any position and succeeds well under trees.

Mid-season :—

SIR JOSEPH PAXTON.—Fruit large, handsome, firm, and of good flavour; heavy cropper; vigorous grower; *forces fairly well ;* a favourite variety with market growers.

Strawberries.

PRESIDENT.—Fruit large, handsome, and of superior flavour; carries well; heavy cropper; robust grower; *good for forcing* and one of the best for main-crop.

FILLBASKET.—Fruit fair size and of excellent flavour; very heavy cropper; requires good culture.

BEDFORD CHAMPION.—Very large fruit of good flavour; vigorous grower; *forces well;* needs good culture.

LAXTON'S REWARD.—Fruit large, firm, and of excellent flavour; heavy cropper, vigorous grower.

DR. HOGG.—Fruit moderate in size, firm, handsome, and of exceptionally fine flavour; fair cropper; compact grower; needs good culture; should not be kept over two years.

Late :—

NEWTON SEEDLING.—Fruit of medium size, firm, good colour and fair quality; very prolific bearer; exceptionally vigorous in growth.

GIVON'S LATE PROLIFIC.—Fruits very large, firm, handsome, and of good flavour; heavy bearer, vigorous grower.

WATERLOO.—Fruit very large, firm, of dark colour and moderate flavour; fair cropper; not very strong in growth.

LAXTON'S LATEST.—Fruit very large, firm, handsome, and of excellent flavour; fair cropper; robust grower.

All the late varieties should be watered while the fruit is swelling.

*Manures :—*Well-decayed farmyard manure is undoubtedly the best manure that can be used for Strawberries, as it not only provides the necessary food for the plant but gives to the soil a greater moisture-retaining power, which is a very important feature in this culture. At the same time it would be a mistake to give heavy dressings to a soil already rich with manure; if it is in high condition the plants may go in without any further manure, but if not, apply from 20 to 40 loads to the acre, the heavier dressing being for the lighter soils, and in addition, 1 to 2 cwt. superphosphate (or 2 to 3 cwt. basic slag), and 3 to 5 cwt. kainit. On soils well manured for the preceding crop the larger quantities of concentrated fertilizers alone will suffice. When growth begins in spring, for each acre mix 2 cwt. superphosphates with 1 cwt. sulphate of potash, and sprinkle this along the sides of the rows, followed a week or two later by a light dusting over the foliage of lime and soot. If growth is backward give ½ cwt. nitrate of soda. Where very large fruit is desired, after the blossom has fallen ring the plants with good guano and water in several times, or give liquid manure between the rows.

19

STRAWBERRIES

I always think myself that strawberries are the most exciting crop of all to grow under cloches. The outdoor strawberry season lasts much too short a time and cloches can double it and at the same time give fruit of superlative quality.

Only about ten or fifteen years ago the old-fashioned tent type of cloche was chiefly used for the strawberry crop but it had many disadvantages, the chief one being that there was never sufficient head-room at the sides of the cloches and the flowers pressed against the glass and were sometimes cut by severe frost. Further, when the cloches were removed to pick the fruit, the foliage of the plants sprang outwards and had to be pressed down again when the glass was put back in position.

The use of barn cloches was a very great improvement, for it meant that there was head-room right up to the edges of the cloches and there was far less risk of damage to the flowers, particularly if a large barn cloche was used. There was still the difficulty that when the cloches were removed in order to pick the fruit, some of the trusses would press out sideways and it was rather a laborious job to put them back under the glass again. The invention of the new panel did away with the necessity for moving the cloches at all. With this new type, the top sheet of glass can be removed, the fruit picked and the glass replaced without disturbing the plants. This is a very great improvement and has made strawberry growing under cloches even more popular than it was before.

The cloche crop is taken as a rule from first-year runners and, in order that the plants should make sufficient growth to yield a decent crop, it is most essential that they should be put out early in the season. If possible, the bed should be prepared in July or

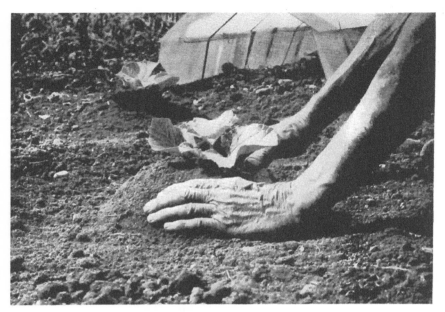

25. Planting out melons

JULY
19th.

26. Capsicums

21

27. Aubergines under cloches raised on adaptor wires

28. *Royal Sovereign 'Malling 40'*

August, but, in a very dry season, the work may have to be postponed until September because the runners need rain when they are first put out. In cloche work you are trying to get early fruit and it is of the greatest importance that an early variety should be used. Strawberries are very prone to virus disease and you should therefore make certain that the runners you buy are from stock certified as 'virus free'. *Royal Sovereign* is an excellent variety and, to my mind, has the best flavour of any. It is also very early and a particular strain called the '*Malling Forty*' is to be recommended. It is very free growing and a good cropper. A great deal of work had been done in the last few years by the Cambridge Plant Breeding Station in producing new seedling varieties suitable for different kinds of work, and these are generally known as *Cambridge* varieties and have been given different numbers. Improvements are being made every year, but, at the time of writing, *Cambridge* 257 and *Cambridge* 173 are two varieties which have proved extremely good for cloche work. They are early, good croppers, of fine flavour and do not make too much leaf.

The first thing to decide is how many cloches and how many runners you require; this of course depends on the crop you wish to pick. A rough estimate is that each barn cloche 2 ft. long will give you about 1 lb. of early strawberries so that the average small gardener would probably be content with a row of ten cloches. With low or large barns I recommend a double row of runners under each row of cloches, the two rows being 8 in. apart and the plants spaced 9 in. apart and staggered so that each plant gets as much room as possible for development. This means that a row of ten barn cloches will take fifty-two runners which is the number that you should order. Your supplier, if he is a good man, will not send you the runners until the weather is rather wet because they do not lift successfully from very dry ground. You cannot therefore be quite sure when the runners are going to arrive and it is essential that you should have prepared your bed beforehand.

It is not absolutely essential that your site should be right out in the open, but there should be no shade from the south side or the fruit will not ripen so readily. Prepare a strip of ground 2 ft. wide by working farmyard manure or compost into the top 6 in. at the rate of a bucketful to the yard run. Before the runners are put out, water thoroughly unless there has been a good shower. Make sure that the runners are firmly planted, and that their growing points are above soil level. They are not of course covered at the time of planting; the earliest time for cloching your row is in December when the plants have been able to make a really good root system during the autumn months. I do not think you should cloche the whole of your row at the same time. If you cover half in December and the other half late in March you will get a succession of fruit for about five weeks before the outdoor crop is ready to pick. If you cannot spare the cloches as early as this, you could cover half your row at the beginning of March and the other half at the beginning of April; this again would give you a succession, but the fruit would all be rather later. Keep the cloches in position over the plants until picking is finished, ventilating them at the top as soon as a warm spell sets in. Do not close them up again unless there is a threat of night frost. In late March or early April, it is a good plan to give a feed of liquid manure.

Some people think that under cloches the flowers will not be properly pollinated. This is not so for it is small beetles rather than bees which pollinate strawberries and there are plenty of these under the cloches. In practice too it is found that bees can always effect an entrance into the cloche rows even if the ventilators are kept shut.

It is not absolutely essential to straw down cloched strawberries as the fruit keeps very clean under the glass. In any case do not put down the straw too early for it seems to reduce the protection which the cloches give. The reason is that it is a non-conductor of heat and it prevents the sun's rays from striking the soil and warming it up. This is what keeps the temperature under the cloches up at night and, if late spring frosts occur, prevents damage to the flowers under the cloches. Straw also attracts slugs, so if you are going to put it down it is better to chop it up into short lengths of 2 in. or 3 in. Slugs will not crawl over the sharp ends and there is of course no danger of the straw being blown away because the cloches prevent this. Some people use dry horticultural peat instead of straw, but there is again the objection that it is an insulator which slightly reduces the protection given by the cloche. The latest material to be used for the purpose is glass wool. It allows the sun's rays to penetrate and is everlasting and at the end of each season it can be boiled up in a mild disinfectant to prevent it from carrying disease or pests. Strawberry mats are also obtainable with a hole in the middle that will slip over the plant and keep the fruit off the soil. These are quite successful and are sometimes used on outdoor crops by market growers.

In a warm spring, picking from under cloches may begin in the home counties as early as the end of April, but ordinarily it will probably be the first week in May before the first good picking is made. If the weather is dry, a good watering is essential. This should be given outside the cloches where it will find its way into the ground and so to the roots of the plants without actually wetting the foliage or the fruit.

Although the largest and earliest fruits are obtained from first-year plants, there are few amateur gardeners who will not want their strawberry bed to last at least a second season. When the plants have finished fruiting at the end of their first season, one row should be removed and scrapped. I do not recommend trying to move the plants to another site; they do not take kindly to transplanting after the first year. It is true that the remaining row will have the plants spaced nine inches apart and this is often considered rather close for second-year plants. I believe, however, that there is no objection to this close spacing and that it will give a larger crop than having the plants much farther apart.

After fruiting, remove all runners, as the formation of runners will undoubtedly weaken the plant. About mid-June, give a good mulch of compost, surrounding the plants to a distance of about 6 in. on each side and giving a depth of 2 in. or 3 in. of compost. This will feed the plants and build them up for next year and is the finest thing possible for them. They will need no further treatment until next spring, except that the beds must be kept weeded. Many people do not cloche their second-year plants, but there is really no reason why they should not do so ; it will save netting and give earlier fruit. Probably a larger cloche will be required because the plants will be a great deal bigger than they were when they were maidens. I do not think it is necessary to cover them until the beginning of April when cloches are usually free from other crops. This will give fruit about a week or ten days earlier than if the plants had never been protected, and it will obviate the necessity for using nets to protect the fruit from birds.

If after fruiting in the second year the plants are still vigorous and free from virus, there is no reason why they should not continue for a third year, this time to grow as outdoor strawberries. If this is the intention they should be given a further dressing of compost after they have finished fruiting and in their third year they will be uncovered and provide main crop strawberries. If they still remain healthy after the third year, which is quite probable if year by year they are given the good compost recommended, there is no reason why they should not go on for a number of years, but as soon as it is found that the yield is diminishing the bed should be scrapped.

My personal preference is to grow the strawberries for three years and to put down a fresh bed every year. This may seem somewhat extravagant if it means buying four dozen runners or more every season. There is no reason, however, why the amateur should not grow his own runners, but for this purpose special plants should be set aside and those which are used for fruiting should not be expected to make runners too. If there is plenty of room in the garden, buy half a dozen virus-free runners —there is no real necessity to get them before October—and plant them out 3 ft. by 3 ft. in ground which has been well prepared with plenty of compost forked into the top 6 in. As soon as the plants are put in, give them a good mulch and when the runners appear in the spring, lead them all into the 6 ft. by 3 ft. rectangle which the six plants will make and peg them down with little wire pegs. You can allow up to ten runners to form on each plant. When these have formed, stop all other runners so that the vigour of the plants goes into the sixty or so which have already been produced. These runners will now be ready to make up your first-year strawberry bed in July or August. Scrap the parent plants and buy another half-dozen runners for producing your plants for next season. In this way you will always be buying new stock and therefore new vigour and reducing the chance of your stock getting virus disease.

Do not forget that one of your objects in cloching your strawberries is to extend the season. It is just as important to extend it at the end as at the beginning. To this end, in addition to the variety which you are going to use for cloche work, you should also plant a late variety which will never be cloched at all. Two good late varieties are *Huxley* and *Tardive de Leopold* and some of the Cambridge seedlings are also good for late cropping. There is no reason why you should not raise your own runners from half a dozen bought in of these late varieties, also using exactly the same procedure. Do not allow old stocks of strawberries to remain in your garden when they no longer bear well as they are likely to harbour strawberry aphis and carry virus to your stocks which are otherwise free. Alpine strawberries are particularly susceptible to virus, so if you must grow them, keep them as far away from your main strawberry beds as possible.

One last tip on strawberry growing. If you can include up to 25 per cent of pine needles in the compost heap which is to be used for growing your strawberries, you will get fruit of exceptional size and flavour.

Ingram Content Group UK Ltd.
Milton Keynes UK
UKHW042205230423
420634UK00022B/161